Conway Album Quilt

(I'm Not From Baltimore)

Patterns and Techniques for Prize-Winning Applique

by Irma Gail Hatcher

Editor's Note: *As this book went to press, the **Conway Album (I'm Not From Baltimore) Quilt,** won two awards at the American International Quilt Show in Houston: first place for Innovative Applique - large quilt and the prestigious Founder's Award.*

Introduction

Making a Baltimore Album quilt has always had mixed appeal for me. I love designing my own blocks, but making red and green blocks with roses that have ten shaded petals does not appeal to me. Also, I prefer more structure in a quilt than simply setting blocks side by side and putting a border around them. Don't get me wrong—I think Baltimore Album quilts are absolutely beautiful! I just don't want to make one, at least not like the ones we traditionally think of as Baltimore Album. I may want to make one someday, but not now.

When planning my *Conway Album* quilt, there were several rules which I imposed upon myself. There would be four predominantly blue blocks (since blue is my favorite color), four predominantly pink or red blocks, and four multicolored blocks. These twelve blocks, set on point, would surround a center medallion block, which would be the equivalent of four blocks in size. The set for the quilt would be similar to a quilt I saw in *America's Glorious Quilts* by Dennis Duke and Deborah Harding. It is a centennial quilt pieced and appliqued by G. Knappenberger in 1876.

Colors for the *Conway Album* were selected by using a "theme fabric." In addition to the colors found in the "theme fabric", I used lighter and darker values of these colors. Each block has some of this "theme fabric", and each block has a three-dimensional aspect to the applique such as stuffed flowers, yo-yo's, folded flowers, gathered flowers, or ruching. Of the eight blue and pink blocks, four are horse-shoe shaped and the other four are circular. The remaining four blocks are a bow-tied bouquet, a cornucopia filled with flowers, a basket filled with flowers, and some kind of "princess feather" design. The applique designs are my own and have only a few pattern pieces for each block.

Making the blocks was fun. I designed each one as I went along. After the blocks were finished, I began to make the center. Including flowers from the blocks in the center area gave continuity to the whole quilt. Since I knew the outside borders would have swags, I also included them in the center. I tried to use the same fabrics in the center which I had used in the blocks, again adding continuity. The biggest decision I had to make in creating this quilt was whether to include the sawtooth border around the blocks. The quilt really looked good without it. But I wanted it so badly. Therefore, it is there.

Irma Gail Hatcher

Irma Gail Hatcher

Bibliography

Dennis Duke and Deborah Harding: *America's Glorious Quilts;* 1987, Park Lane, New York, p. 47.

Jeana Kimball: *Red and Green - An Applique Tradition;* 1990, That Patchwork Place, Inc., Bothell, Washington.

Maggie Malone: *Heirloom Quilts You Can Make;* 1984, Sterling Publishing Co., Inc., New York.

Elly Sienkiewicz: *Baltimore Beauties and Beyond, Volume One;* 1989, C & T Publishing, Lafayette, California.

Elly Sienkiewicz: *Baltimore Beauties and Beyond, Volume Two;* 1989, C & T Publishing, Lafayette, California.

Elly Sienkiewicz: *Baltimore Album Quilts;* 1990, C & T Publishing, Lafayette, California.

How To Use This Book

There are many ways in which this book may be used. One can make a replica of this quilt or it can be used simply as a reference book.

The twelve individual blocks, plus one more, can be used to make a more traditional Baltimore Album style quilt, see Layout A, or an individual block will make a beautiful pillow. The large center block and four of the 12" blocks along with a border can be used to make a wall hanging, Layout B.

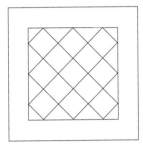
Layout A

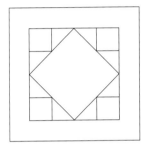
Layout B

You may want to change the blocks; just because I put pansies in the basket, doesn't mean you can't put daisies. Whatever option you choose, if you can imagine it, you can do it with the techniques presented in this book. By learning these and other techniques you greatly enhance your abilities to be a creative quilter.

It is my sincere wish that the readers of this book will find some new and interesting ways to add a personal touch to their quilts. It is my hope to show that one does not need to be an artist to make up applique patterns. The patterns shown in this book were made by cutting paper and are very simple, using the same pattern over and over again in a single block.

Included in this book are General Directions for the following techniques used to make this quilt.

Please read these General Directions carefully before beginning to make this quilt. Reading them may help to eliminate some problems that might occur later on.

1. **How to Choose Fabrics and Fabric Requirements** *for entire quilt, page 4.*

2. **Making Templates and Marking the Background Fabric.** *Directions for making plastic templates, pages 4 and 5.*

3. **Basic Applique.** *The "finger press" method of applique and how to make perfect points, page 5.*

4. **Flat Circles & Ovals.** *Perfectly round and smooth circles achieved with cardboard and spray starch, page 6.*

5. **Bias Strips.** *Multiple strips of bias are drawn at one time, page 6.*

6. **Yo-Yos.** *Old and new ways to use this three dimensional piece, page 6.*

7. **Stuffed Circles.** *How to make grapes or the centers of flowers, page 7.*

8. **Folded Rosebud.** *Creating delicate, three dimensional rosebuds, page 7.*

9. **Ruching.** *Detailed instructions for making ruched flowers and the basket detailing, pages 7 and 8.*

10. **Applique with Trapunto.** *Trapunto adds a three dimensional look to an appliqued flower, page 8.*

11. **Gathered Flower.** *Cutting the center area of a petal wider than the pattern, then gathering the area can give a three-dimensional look to any flower which has petals, page 9.*

12. **Broderie Perse.** *Also known as "Persian Embroidery", Broderie Perse is a technique used in the Peacock Block. Little clusters of flowers which were cut from printed fabric are appliqued in place. However, any size flower could be used, page 9.*

13. **Sawtooth Border.** *Make 440 square units of two triangles in about 3 hours or less, pages 9 and 10. If one chooses not to include the fast-pieced triangle border, a separate Pattern C on page 14 has been included for the large aqua triangles.*

14. **Dogtooth Border.** *Directions included for making the appliqued border which surrounds the center and outside of the quilt, pages 10 and 11.*

15. **Finishing Your Quilt.** *Joining the blocks, adding borders, quilting ideas, and attaching the binding are all discussed beginning on page 48.*

General Directions and Techniques

How to Choose Fabrics

Every piece of fabric used in the Conway Album quilt is 100% cotton and is a print except for the off-white muslin which is a solid. Using blends was out of the question since the "finger press" method of applique was employed. First chosen was a "theme fabric," a fabric which had all of the colors I wanted to use in the quilt. The fabric didn't have many dark valued colors in it; therefore, I added quite a few. It did have peachy pink, periwinkle blue, light golden yellow, and blue green.

When darker peachy pinks were added, they turned into shades of burgundy; when lighter shades of burgundy were used, they turned into rosier colors. All of these pink colors seemed to look right together and were all used. There are about nine different pinks in the quilt. There are about seven different blues, shaded from light to dark; however, the dark blue is still periwinkle and not navy. Only two yellow fabrics are included, one slightly darker than the other. The "theme fabric" has an allover yellowish-tan appearance. Two brown fabrics were used in addition to several lighter shades of brown for the cornucopia.

Many greens were used, twenty-one to be exact. I had been collecting greens for another quilt. The greens which I had collected all had some dark bluegreen in them. Several also had yellow green with the bluegreen. There aren't any which are bright; they all have a little black in them. I also added some medium blue greens to blend in with the aqua used to set the quilt together.

The aqua print fabric was not chosen until several blocks had been made. At first I had chosen a dark pink fabric—six yards of it. But when the blocks were teamed up with it, the different pinks began to fight, and it did nothing for the blues. When the aqua was set side by side with the blocks, the pinks settled down and the blues began to glow. I must admit that I learned a lot about color while making this quilt. But isn't that why we keep making quilts, one after another?

When selecting fabrics, I tried to vary the kind of prints used—small flowery prints, large flowery prints, geometric prints, plaids, paisleys, pin dots, small leafy prints, large leafy prints, etc. In most cases I used prints which had only two colors in them. I have used many two color prints since reading Jinny Beyer's book, *Medallion Quilts*. These kinds of prints can be used with almost any third color. Buying fabrics with several colors in them limits their use. I do buy multi-color prints and use the two color prints to go with them, which is what I have done in this quilt. The "theme fabric" is a multi-color print, and the fabrics chosen to go with it are two color prints.

Fabric Requirements for Conway Album Quilt:

1 yd "theme" (floral print) fabric
6 1/2 yds aqua print
8 1/2 yds off-white muslin
1/4 yd each or scraps of 9 shades pink to burgundy
1/4 yd each or scraps of 7 shades blue lt to med dk
3/4 yd yellow print
1/2 yd each of 13 dk green prints for stems and leaves
1/4 yd each or scraps of 8 other greens
1/4-1/2 yd brown print
scraps of 4 other shades of lt brown for cornucopia
9 yds backing

Making Templates and Marking Background Fabric

For each block, trace patterns from this book onto tracing paper, placing patterns as close together as possible. Count the number of times the pattern is used in the block and write this number on tissue paper. Also write the color needed and name of the block on each pattern piece. Using a glue stick, cover all of the patterns on the tissue paper. Place sticky side of tissue on top of template plastic and smooth in place. Cut out patterns. **Note:** *These patterns do not include seam allowance.*

On the wrong side of the background (off-white muslin) fabric, mark with pencil, twelve 12" squares leaving at least 1" between squares; make sure they are drawn on the straight grain of fabric. Pencil lines will later be used as seam lines. Cut out 12 1/2" squares.

Using the corner points of the lines drawn, find the center of each side. Fold the square down the middle using these center points, and press crease in the fabric. Fold square the other way using the other center points, and press a crease, being careful not to press over the crease previously made. Also, make folds on the diagonals, using opposite corners, and press creases, making sure not to press over creases previously made. If the fabric has been creased correctly, all of the crease marks will meet in the same point in the center of the block. Let fabric completely cool. Repeat this process for the 34 1/2" center square and 12" x 96" border strips.

Using a water soluble marking pen, mark the 12 1/2" squares, 34 1/2" center square, and 12" x 96" border strips on the right side. **Note**: *Marking pens should always be tested with each fabric first to make sure that they can be washed out.* Never use an ordinary pencil; some antique quilts still have pencil markings after 100 years. Draw patterns onto background fabric, using the templates you have made, positioning them according to the block layout given with each block and border strip. Pattern pieces should not come closer than 1/2" to the seam line. The crease lines should help you place patterns correctly. There are no patterns for the stems since they will be made from bias strips.

A fold-up 36" x 72" cardboard cutting board with a grid, which can be purchased at most sewing supply stores or discount stores, is useful in marking large size pieces such as the center block and outside borders of this quilt.

Basic Applique

I use the finger press method of applique, which I learned from Nancy Pearson. I like this method because, when I am ready to applique, I can just begin. I don't have to use the iron, or baste anything.

First, draw the entire design onto background fabric using templates and following the layout for each square and border strip.

Then each pattern piece, without seam allowance, is drawn on the right side of the fabric (as listed in Fabric Requirements for each section) on the bias, **Fig 1**; be sure to leave space between each pattern piece to allow for seam allowances. Always cut pieces on the bias, especially if there are points or other difficult areas to applique. When cutting the fabric, add 1/8" seam allowance, unless otherwise specified, to each pattern piece. The seam allowance is then folded under and finger pressed a little at a time around the whole piece, being careful not to stretch the edge of the piece. The piece is positioned onto the marked background fabric and appliqued in place, with matching thread, and stitched with 10 to 12 stitches per inch. If I need to pin a piece in position, I pin from the back so that the thread does not get caught on the pin.

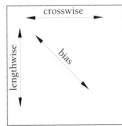

Fig 1

Before taking the first stitch, hide the knot in the folded seam allowance of the piece to be appliqued in an area where there are no points. For each stitch, hold the needle perpendicular, **Fig 2**, to the edge of the applique; insert needle under applique 1/16" into the background fabric; twist and turn needle so that needle comes up in the fold of the applique. A right handed person should stitch in a counter clockwise direction over the top of the applique, **Fig 3**.

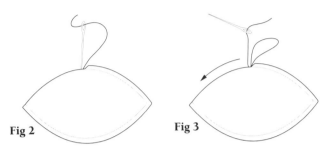

Fig 2   Fig 3

When a point is reached, stitch right to the point, and bring the needle out of the fold at the point, **Fig 4**. With right hand fold a little of the seam allowance under on the other side of the point, **Fig 5**. Hold in place with left hand and finger press hard; pull thread to make sure point was not folded under. Fold rest of seam allowance under, hold in place with left hand, and pull thread again to make sure point wasn't turned under.

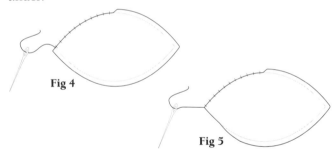

Fig 4

Fig 5

When seam allowance is turned under and there is a nice point, take a small stitch into the background fabric (about 1/32") to achieve an even more "pointy" look and continue stitching. Continue in same manner until entire piece is appliqued.

When the ends of stems or leaves, etc. are going to be covered by another piece of applique, excess fabric should be cut away and seam allowances opened so that the area will be flat under the piece to be appliqued, **Fig 6**.

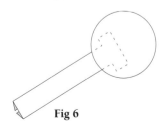

Fig 6

Flat Circles and Ovals

For making circles or ovals use the spray starch method. Cut a cardboard oval or circle to the exact desired size. Be careful to cut the cardboard smoothly so that the edge of the circle is without ridges. Cut fabric about 3/8" larger than the cardboard and draw up around the cardboard with a basting stitch close to the edge; leave a long tail of thread. Spray cardboard and fabric with spray starch on both sides. Iron on the back with a hot iron, turn over and iron on the front. Dry completely, then remove the cardboard. Pull thread tail to draw the piece back into the flat shape. Cut the thread tail and applique the piece in place with same stitch as in Basic Applique, page 5. Correctly done, the little circles or ovals do not have ridges and are easily stitched in place. The seam allowance acts as a kind of stuffing which makes the circle or oval look 3-dimensional. For a more 3-dimensional effect, two or three layers of cotton batting can be inserted as the piece is appliqued. It is important to remember that anything added will give a 3-dimensional effect. If too much is added, edge of applique will pucker and not wear as well.

Bias Strips

Bias strips are cut, of course, on the bias. Nancy Pearson taught me to draw several at a time, enough for the whole block, before cutting them out. All bias strips are 1/4" finished.

First a line is drawn on the bias of the fabric. One-eighth of an inch from that line, another line is drawn. Another line is drawn 1/4 inch from the second line; the next lines are drawn 1/8"; 1/8", 1/4", 1/8"; 1/8", 1/4", 1/8"; etc. The 1/2" strips are then cut as indicated in **Fig 7.**

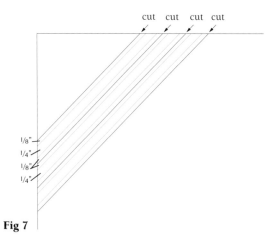

Fig 7

Yo-Yos

When cutting circles for yo-yos, decide what size diameter is needed for the finished yo-yo and then double it and add 1/8". For example, for a 2" diameter finished yo-yo, cut a 4 1/8" (2"+2"+1/8") diameter circle. When the correct size is determined, cut out the circle, **Fig 8.** Hold the circle with wrong side of fabric facing you, turn over 1/8" seam allowance, and stitch using a running stitch with matching thread. The running stitches should alternate from 1/8" to 1/4" to 1/8" to 1/4", etc. in length, all around the circle as close to the edge as possible, **Fig 9.** When the circle has been stitched, pull the thread, **Fig 10** and push the seam allowance side to the inside of the yo-yo, **Fig 11.** When the stitches are done in this manner, the yo-yo lies flat, the gathers are even, and the hole in the center is small. If the stitches are all even and small, the hole in the center will be large. If the stitches are not sewn very close to the edge, a little ridge forms around the hole when the thread is pulled. Adjust the gathers and position the hole in the center. Push needle down to the back side of the yo-yo, and knot the thread on the back. Applique in place.

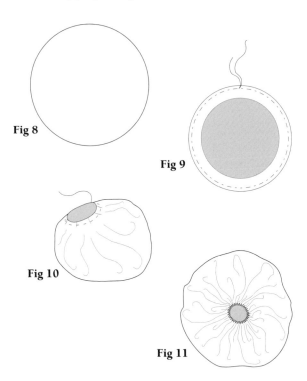

Fig 8

Fig 9

Fig 10

Fig 11

In some of the blocks a small yo-yo is appliqued in place upside down for a 3-dimensional effect. For this kind of yo-yo, one would not knot the thread on the back, but on the front.

Stuffed Circles

Cut circle twice the diameter of the desired finished circle. For example, a finished 2" circle is cut 4" in diameter. Hand sew around the edge 1/4" from edge. Before pulling the thread, put a small amount of stuffing in the center and pull the thread, **Fig 12.** Position circle on background fabric in proper place. Applique with very tiny stitches (see Basic Applique on page 5), making sure that edge of the circle follows the line drawn on the background fabric exactly. If circle doesn't quite touch line, push the circle with fingernail until it touches and stitch in place. If the circle seems too large for the circle drawn on the background, push under circle fabric with needle until line can be seen and stitch in place, **Fig 13.** If circle is sewn in this manner, with the edge of the circle touching every part of the line drawn on the background fabric, perfect stuffed circles will be the result. Remember the lines on the background fabric are there for us to follow.

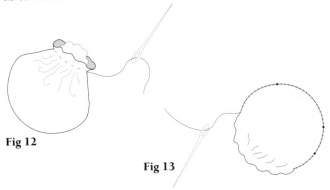

Fig 12

Fig 13

Folded Rosebud

For rosebud, cut a 3 1/2" diameter circle of fabric. With wrong sides together fold circle in half, **Fig 14.** Fold again on lines shown in **Fig 15.** Baste along sides and top edges, **Fig 16,** with thread that doesn't match. Do not clip thread. Turn bud over and cut away back layer of fabric as shown, **Fig 17.** Turn over to front again. Make two little pleats in lower edge and baste in place, **Fig 18.** Position on background, and applique in place with matching thread. Sew across bottom edge of bud, securing pleats so that bud's green sepal will cover the stitching. Remove basting thread.

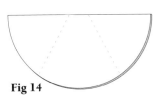

Fig 14

Fig 15

Fig 16

Fig 17

Fig 18

Ruching

When choosing fabrics to be ruched, large prints, plaids, stripes, and geometric prints look wonderful. In fact, I have yet to see a fabric which wasn't beautiful when ruched.

Ruching in this quilt requires strips that are one inch wide, cut on the lengthwise or crosswise grain of the fabric. Fold raw edges of the strip lengthwise toward center so that they meet in the back. The one inch strip folds to a 1/2" strip.

Use strong quilting thread, if possible, the same color as the fabric. Start in the upper right edge of the strip, with knot on the back, and stitch in a 45 degree angle direction. When stitching is near the lower edge of the strip, bring needle to the top and over the edge, bringing needle up from the back. Continue to stitch so that stitching lines form right angles along the strip, **Fig 19.**

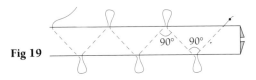

Fig 19

It is important to form "right" or 90 degree angles each time so that the ruched strip will be the same width. This will be particularly important when making the ruching for the basket. If "V"-shaped angles are formed, the strip width will be narrow; if wide "obtuse" angles are formed, the strip width will be wide. Drawing the stitching lines on the strip will aid in making the correct angle, **Fig 20;** or cutting a corner triangle from a piece of paper so that the base of the triangle is 1/2" from the 90 degree angle, **Fig 21.** This little triangle can then be held on top of the strip as you are stitching to aid in making the right angles, **Fig 22.**

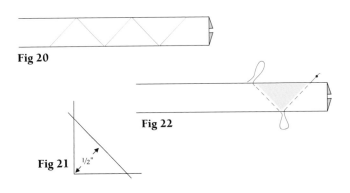

Fig 20

Fig 22

Fig 21   1/2"

Continue ruching in this manner for four inches; pull thread. Notice that the stitching line forms a straight line down the center of the strip when the thread is pulled. Arrange gathers. The edges of the ruching should have definite scallops and should not be pulled too tightly, **Fig 23.**

Fig 23

When ruching is about 10" long, thread another needle. Hold ruching in left hand, turn end down and around in a clockwise direction, tucking the end under the ruching; tack in place with second needle, **Fig 24.** Do not cut thread.

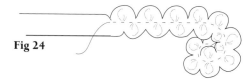

Fig 24

Bring first petal up on top of ruching so that the edge of the petal touches the center of the ruching strip below it. Stab stitch the petal in place with the second needle. Continue turning in clockwise manner and tack each petal in place with a stab stitch, **Fig 25.** Don't force petals to be in a certain place. Just let their edges follow the ruching center line, and tack the petals where they fall, making sure that the flower lies flat.

Fig 25

Continue ruching and securing petals with two different needles until the desired size flower is reached. Don't ruche too far ahead or you may have to take stitches out. When the desired size is reached, ruche just enough more so that the tail end can be tucked under the flower. Pull ruching thread until it gathers correctly and tie off; cut thread and trim excess strip. Tuck tail under flower and secure in place with other thread, **Fig 26.** Tie off thread.

Fig 26

Position flower in place and applique, taking 10 to 12 stitches per inch around the outside edge. When the outside edge of the flower is stitched in place, stitch each interior

petal down using approximately 3 stab stitches per petal to hold in place. Make the stab stitches in the folds of the petals so that the stitches don't show. Tie off thread. Appliqueing the petals down in this way flattens the flower somewhat, but they should still be on the quilt 100 years from now.

Applique with Trapunto

In the Bow Tied Bouquet Block, page 36, the three red flowers have been appliqued, then stuffed using the trapunto method. After all three flowers have been appliqued, turn over with the wrong side up (you will see the appliqued stitched outline of each flower on the back). Draw a little circle in the middle of each flower on the back side of the piece, **Fig 27.** Draw five more petals around the center circle, **Fig 28.** Draw lines to the outside edge to separate outer petals, **Fig 29.** Sew on each petal line with small running stitches, 10 to 12 per inch, sewing from the back. Turn the piece over to the front. Applique a small yellow stuffed circle (see Stuffed Circles on page 7) to the center of each flower.

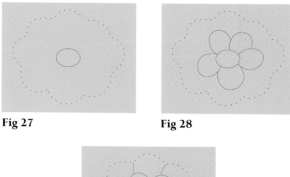

Fig 27   **Fig 28**

Fig 29

Turn the block over to the back again. Using small embroidery scissors, cut small slits in the background fabric only in the middle of each petal, **Fig 30.** (Do not cut the center of each flower where the small stuffed yellow circle has been appliqued.) Stuff each petal, pushing stuffing gently into the opening until area is evenly but lightly stuffed. Too much stuffing will pucker the edge of the applique, or keep the block from lying flat. Just a little stuffing will be enough. Whip stitch slits closed.

Fig 30

Gathered Flowers

The Princess Feather Block, page 15, has a flower which has gathered petals in the center. There are two patterns given for the petal—the one with the narrow base is used to transfer the design onto the background fabric, **Fig 31,** and the one with the wider base is used to cut the pattern pieces from fabric for the petals, **Fig 32.**

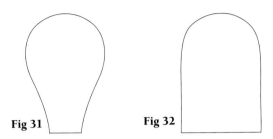

Fig 31   Fig 32

Cut each petal on the bias to make appliqueing easier. Finger press the seam allowance under the entire curved edge of the petal. Do not finger press the seam allowance at the base of the petal. Position the top of the petal with the top of the petal drawn on the background fabric, and begin to applique on the right-hand side of the petal, following the drawn line. Continue to applique toward the left-hand side of the petal. At this point there should be extra fabric sticking up at the base of the petal. Make tiny basting stitches along base, **Fig 33,** and gather so that extra fabric lies flat against the background fabric, **Fig 34.** Tack down in place. Trim extra seam allowance at base of petal.

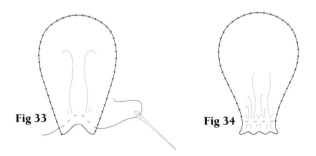

Fig 33   Fig 34

Broderie Perse

In the Peacock Block, page 20, tiny flowers from the "theme fabric" have been cut and appliqued to the leafy areas. However, any size flowers could be used here, not just tiny ones.

Cut flower(s), adding 1/8" seam allowance. Finger press the seam allowance under, and applique in place just as you would any other applique (see Basic Applique on page 5). Smaller flowers are harder to applique because they have so many small inside and outside points. Gently curving petals are easier to applique than the pointy ones. Appliqueing clusters of small flowers would be easier than appliqueing

individual flowers. It is also possible to "round off" the pointy areas, **Fig 35.**

Fig 35

Sawtooth Border

The sawtooth border that frames the individual applique blocks is actually pieced to larger fast-pieced triangles first. This border is optional and the quilt looks beautiful without it. If the sawtooth border is to be omitted, use Pattern C for a larger aqua print triangle.

Making Fast-Pieced Triangles

If the sawtooth border is to be used, photocopy the grid sheet (on page 12) 11 times. Each grid sheet will produce 40 fast-pieced triangles; 424 are needed for the sawtooth border. Cut 11 pieces each of background fabric and aqua print fabric a little bit larger than the grid sheet. Lay one piece of background fabric and one piece of aqua print fabric right sides together. Lay a grid sheet on top of these fabrics, making sure that grain lines of the fabrics are in line with the edge of the grid sheet. Notice that the grid sheet has vertical, horizontal, and diagonal lines. Pin the sheet to the fabrics half way between the diagonal lines, **Fig 36.** With tiny machine stitches, stitch on all dashed lines. When all stitching is completed, cut through the sheet and fabric. First, cut the outside lines; then cut all vertical, horizontal and diagonal lines. Each grid sheet will produce 40 square units which are made up of one background triangle and one aqua print triangle. Remove stitching at points of triangles, **Fig 37.**

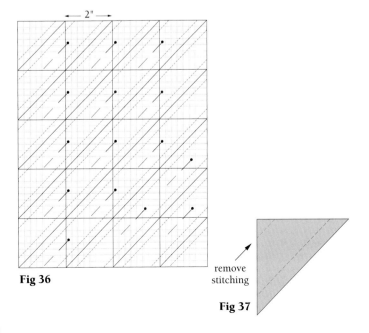

Fig 36

remove stitching

Fig 37

Tear the paper off by tearing from the center of the seam line to the outside edges. Tearing the paper off this way will keep seams from coming apart. Gently finger press seam toward the aqua side, taking care not to stretch the bias seam. Iron seam in place. Continue stitching grid sheets to fabric and cutting them apart until all 11 sheets are finished.

Cut a 1 1/2" square from template plastic. Trim each fast-pieced triangle unit to exactly 1 1/2" square. Being exact here will keep problems from occurring later.

Piecing and Attaching The Sawtooth Border

The Sawtooth Border is pieced and attached to aqua print triangles.

Note: For Patterns A, B, C and D add 1/4" seam allowance when cutting fabric.

Cut 16 Pattern A large aqua triangles. Cut 40 Pattern D small triangles from background fabric.

Sew 10 fast-pieced triangle units together; add one Pattern D triangle to the end, **Fig 38.** Sew to the right side of large Pattern A aqua triangle, **Fig 39.**

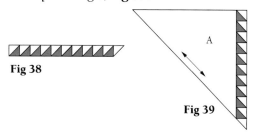

Fig 38

A

Fig 39

Sew 11 triangle units together; add one Pattern D triangle to one end, **Fig 40.** Sew to adjacent side of large Pattern A aqua triangle, **Fig 41.**

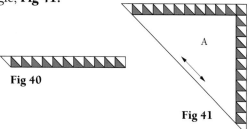

Fig 40

A

Fig 41

Continue sewing triangle units together until 16 Pattern A aqua print triangles are completed.

Cut 8 Pattern B triangles from aqua print fabric; two will be used at each corner.

Sew 11 triangle units together; add one Pattern D triangle to one end, **Fig 42.** Sew to one Pattern B aqua print triangle, **Fig 43.**

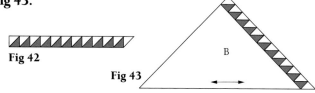

Fig 42

B

Fig 43

Sew 11 triangle units together; add one Pattern D triangle to the end, **Fig 44.** Sew to another Pattern B aqua triangle, **Fig 45.** Set aside for finishing.

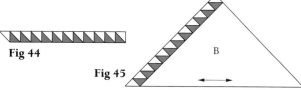

Fig 44

B

Fig 45

Dogtooth Border

The dogtooth borders are the appliqued triangular borders around the center block and each side of the outside border. The secret to having these borders match the Sawtooth Borders around the 12" blocks, is to have the border drawn correctly on the background fabric. I have found that using the grid on a 36" x 72" cardboard cutting board is helpful in both drawing the center block and the outside borders, and is extremely helpful when making accurate dogtooth borders.

Drawing the Dogtooth Border

For Center Square, mark 1/4" seam line, using a water soluble marking pen, along raw edges of 34 1/2" muslin square, **Fig 46.** Using the triangle template (pattern O, page 43), mark the first triangle on the marked seam line at the center point of each edge. Then, draw five triangles on each side of center triangle easing slightly to fit. Repeat on other three edges, **Fig 47. Note:** *There is a half triangle at each corner.*

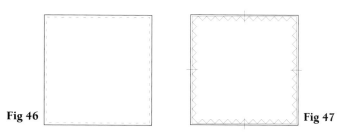

Fig 46

Fig 47

For Outside Border, mark 1/4" seam line along one raw edge (for inner border) of the four 12" x 96" muslin border strips and 1/2" seam line on opposite raw edge (for outer border) of the four border strips. Using the triangle template (Pattern O, page 43), draw the first triangle for the inner border on the marked 1/4" seam line at the center of one long edge of border strip; draw the second triangle 8 1/2" from the center point; the third triangle 17" from center; the fourth triangle 25 1/2" from center; and the fifth, 34" from center, **Fig 48.**

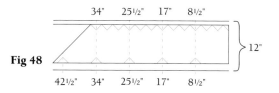

Fig 48

34" 25½" 17" 8½"

12"

42½" 34" 25½" 17" 8½"

Then, draw the triangles in between easing to fit evenly; triangles will overlap slightly. *Note: It is important that triangles are drawn on the marked places (8 1/2", 17", 25 1/2", etc.) first because they will have to match sawtooth borders of the blocks when putting quilt together.*

For outer border, draw triangles on opposite raw edge along 1/2" seam line in same manner as for inner border, except draw triangles to end of strip at 42 1/2", **Fig 48.**

After the pattern for the dogtooth border is drawn on the both the center square and inner and outer edges of border fabric, turn the fabric over to see if the drawn dogtooth border can be seen from the wrong side. If it can't be seen, mark the high points and the low points of the border on the wrong side, **Fig 49.**

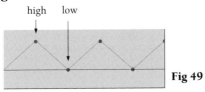
Fig 49

Preparing strips for Dogtooth:

Tear four 2 1/2" x 36" strips along the lengthwise grain of the aqua print fabric for the center square border and eight 2 1/2" x 96" strips for the outside border. Tearing the fabric guarantees that the edges will be straight and on the grain.

Stitching the Dogtooth Border

For Center Block, baste a 36" aqua print strip to the top edge of 34 1/2" muslin square about 1/2" down from drawn dogtooth border. Baste from the back so that you can see the high and low points on the wrong side of the background fabric, **Fig 50.**

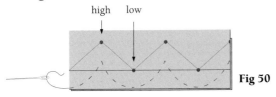
Fig 50

Turn piece over to the right side. When appliqueing the dogtooth border, it is very important to follow the lines drawn on the background fabric. Starting at the right side edge of the border, gently fold the strip back just enough so that the diagonal line for the applique can be seen. This fold should lie right on the diagonal line. Trim excess strip fabric so that only 1/4" is left for a seam allowance, **Fig 51.**

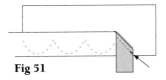
Fig 51

Fold the seam allowance under enough so that the diagonal line on the background fabric is barely visible. Finger press this seam allowance in place, being careful not to stretch fabric. Beginning near the lower edge of the first drawn triangle, applique toward the high point of the border, **Fig 52.**

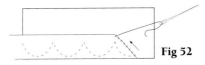
Fig 52

Place a pin through the next low point and cut the strip to this low point, **Fig 53.** Gently fold the fabric back enough so that line on the background fabric can be seen. Trim excess fabric away so that only 1/4" seam allowance is left. You may also need to trim excess seam allowance at the point in order to have a nice, neat, flat point (see Basic Applique on page 5). Fold seam allowance under and fingerpress in place. Applique to the low point, **Fig 54.**

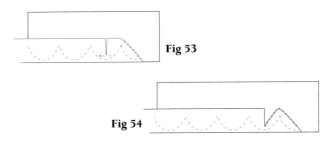
Fig 53

Fig 54

Fold back fabric enough so that diagonal line to the next high point can be seen. Trim excess fabric away so that only 1/4" seam allowance is left. Fold seam allowance under and finger press in place. You may need to take an extra stitch in the low point to keep fabric threads from fraying. Applique to the high point. Continue appliqueing in this manner until the border on each side is complete.

Applique dogtooth border on inner and outer edges of marked border strips in same manner using the 2 1/2" x 96" aqua print strips. Clipping the background fabric behind the dogtooth border is optional. I did not clip mine. I wanted that extra strength to keep the outside edges of the quilt from stretching.

2"

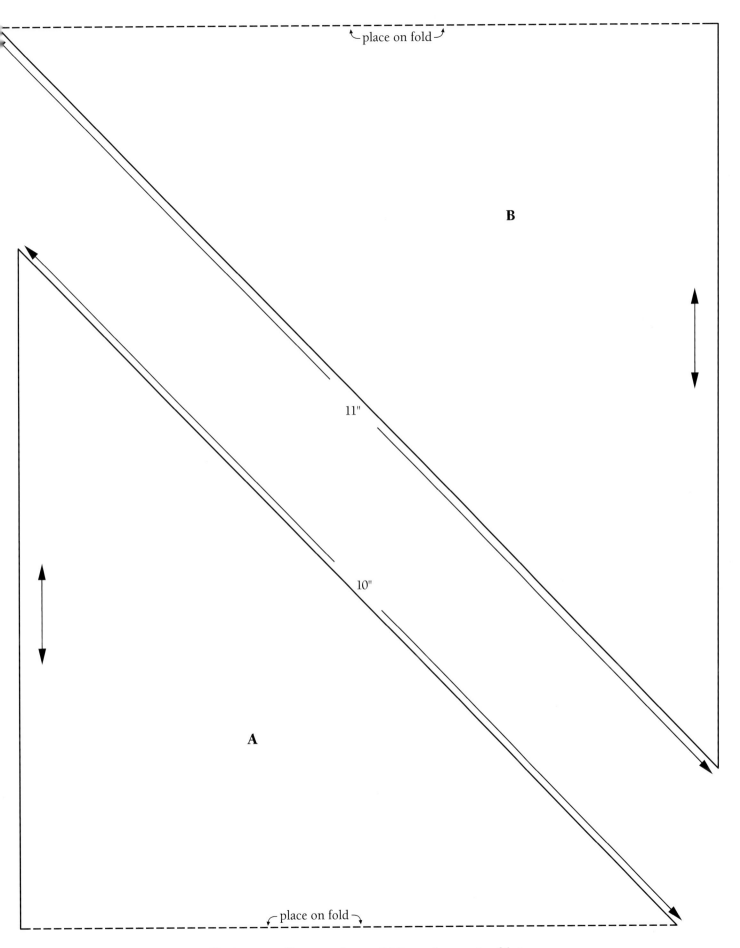

place on fold

B

11"

10"

A

place on fold

Add 1/4" seam allowance along solid lines when cutting fabric.

13

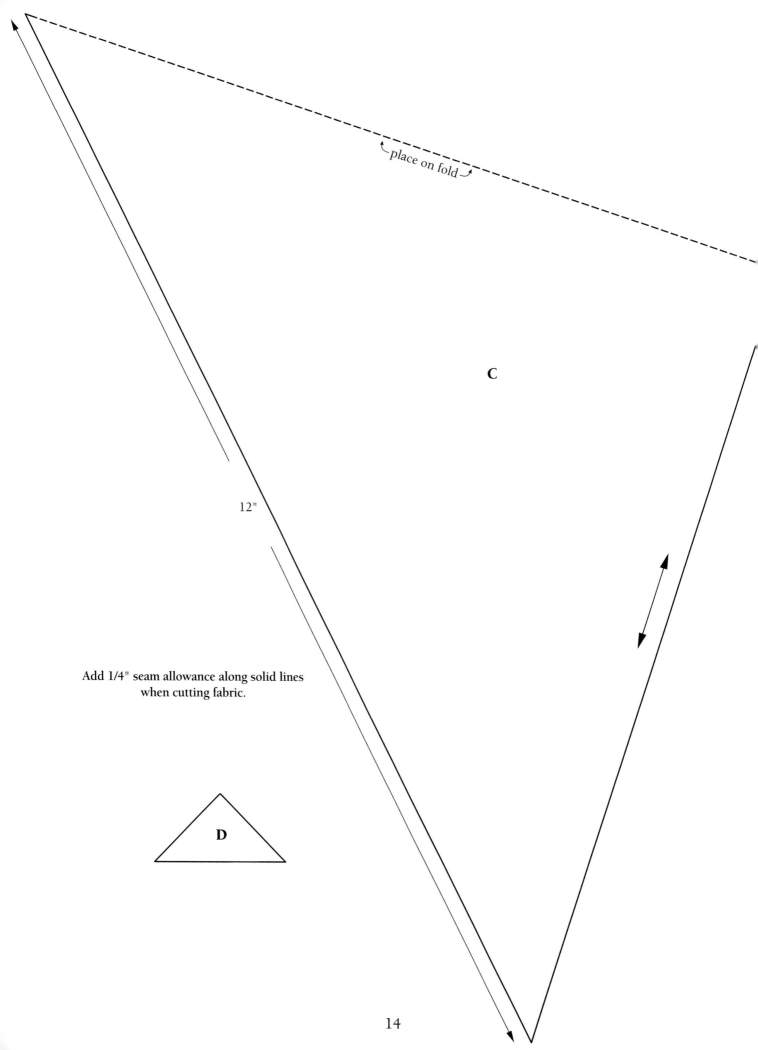

place on fold

C

12"

Add 1/4" seam allowance along solid lines
when cutting fabric.

D

Princess Feather

Shown in color on page 23

This block has a 3-dimensional flower with gathered petals and a stuffed center. It is surrounded by large flowing leaves and colorful berries.

Materials:

12 1/2" square for background
theme fabric for stems
four green fabrics for leaves
lt pink fabric for petals of flower
dk pink fabric for center of flower
med pink fabric for berries
thread to match each fabric

Patterns

A leaf, cut 4
B petal, cut 5
C berry, cut 12
D flower center, cut 1
E flower center placement
F petal placement

Instructions:

Note: *See Basic Applique, page 5, before beginning to applique.*

1. Trace all pattern pieces onto template plastic (see Making Templates on page 4).

2. Mark design on background square (see Marking Background Fabric on page 4). **Note:** *Use patterns E and F only to mark design on background square.*

3. Cut out pattern pieces A through D from fabric adding 1/8" seam allowance all around.

4. Finger press leaves and applique in place.

5. Cut bias strips for stems (see Bias Strips on page 6). Finger press each side and applique along drawn line. Cut excess strip.

6. Applique flower petals in place (see Gathered Flowers on page 9).

7. Applique stuffed circle in place at center of flower (see Stuffed Circles on page 7).

8. Applique berries in place.

Block Layout

continued

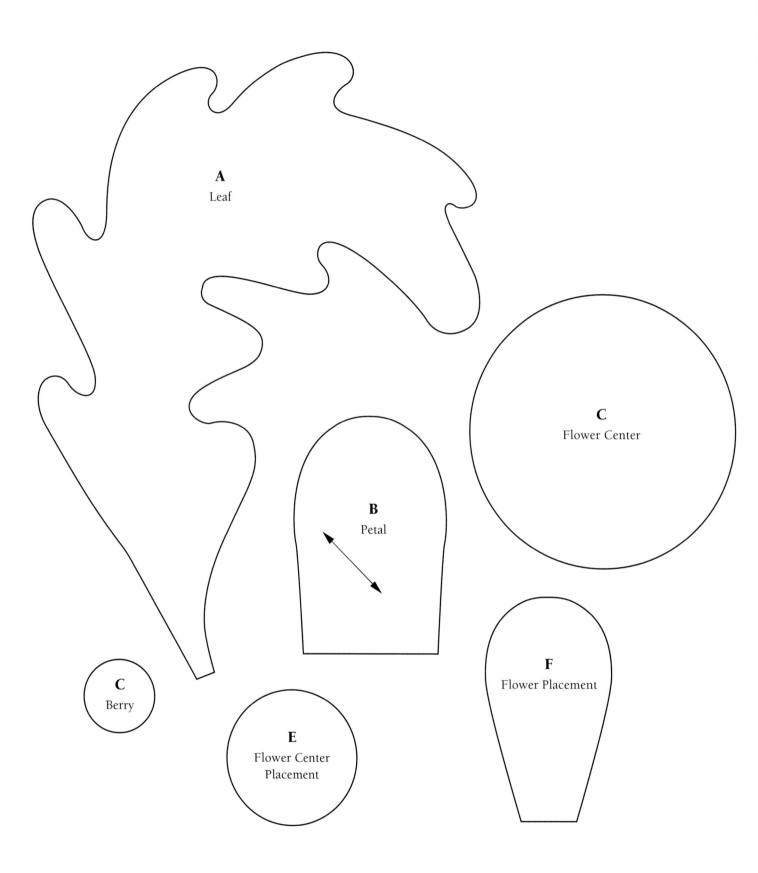

A
Leaf

C
Flower Center

B
Petal

F
Flower Placement

C
Berry

E
Flower Center
Placement

Texas Bluebonnets

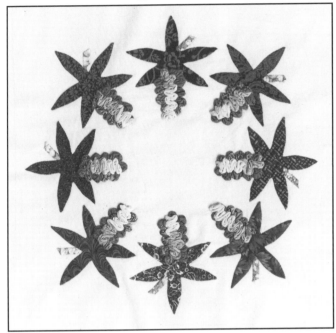

Shown in color on page 23

A small bias strip for the stem, a five-pointed leaf, and another ruched strip make up this block. The ruched strip actually has five shades of blue sewn together to make one long strip.

Materials:
12 1/2" muslin square for background
bias strips for stems (theme fabric)
assorted green fabrics
five shades (light to dark) of blue fabrics
matching thread

Patterns:
A leaf, cut 8
B Bluebonnet placement

Instructions:

Note: *See Basic Applique, page 5, before beginning to applique.*

1. Trace pattern pieces onto template plastic (see Making Templates on page 4).

2. Mark design on background square (see Marking Background Fabric on page 4). Use pattern B to mark placement of Bluebonnets.

3. Cut out pattern piece A from fabric adding 1/8" seam allowance all around.

4. Applique all stems (see Bias Strips, page 6).

5. Applique all leaves.

6. For ruched Bluebonnet, cut eight 1" x 5" strips from each blue fabric. Make eight stacks of blue fabric strips, each stack containing one each of the five different shades of blue fabric. These should be stacked from light to dark.

7. Place first strip right side up and second strip, right side down at a right angle; stitch diagonal seam, **Fig 1.** Place next strip at a right angle to second strip and stitch in same manner. Continue adding strips until the final and darkest strip is added, **Fig 2.** Trim seams; press open.

Fig 1

Fig 2

8. Fold lengthwise edges of completed strip to the center and press flat. Ruche strip (see Ruching on pages 7 and 8). When the whole strip has been ruched, tie off thread and tuck each end under; tack in place. **Note:** *Do not tack as for ruched flower at this time.*

9. Make a U-Shape starting at the darker end of strip, **Fig 3.** Tack in place by sewing between the two sides.

10. Fold up the lighter ruched section, so that this section covers the middle of the U-Shape part of the flower, **Fig 4.** Tack in place.

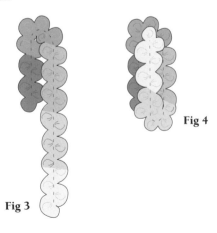

Fig 4

Fig 3

11. Applique ruched Bluebonnet in place.

17

continued

Block Layout

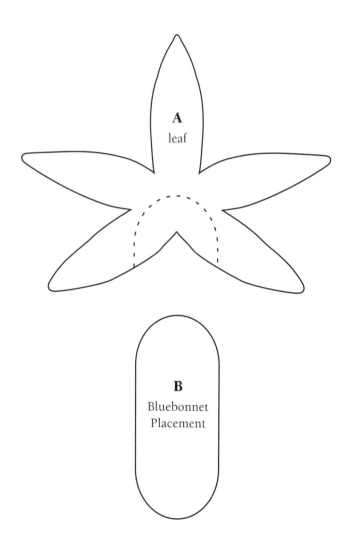

A
leaf

B
Bluebonnet
Placement

Rose of Sharon with Rosebuds

Shown in color on page 23

This block has six pattern pieces, plus a bias strip used for the stem. The buds have a 3-dimensional look which was achieved by folding fabric.

Materials:

12 1/2" muslin square for background
dk green bias strips for stems, 16" and 12" long
assorted green fabrics for leaves
brown fabric for sepals
dk pink for Pattern B, med pink for Pattern A, and theme fabric for Pattern C
theme fabric for rosebuds
matching thread

Patterns:

A outside flower, cut 1
B middle flower, cut 1
C flower center, cut 1
D rosebuds, cut 5
E sepal, cut 5
F leaf, cut 13
G rosebud placement

Instructions:

Note: *See Basic Applique on page 5 before beginning to applique.*

1. Trace pattern pieces onto template plastic (see Making Templates on page 4).

2. Mark design on background square (see Marking Background Fabric on page 4). Use pattern G to mark rosebud placement.

3. Cut out pattern pieces A through F from fabric adding 1/8" seam allowance all around.

4. Cut bias strips (see Bias Strips on page 6). Finger press seam allowance under; applique in place.

5. Applique all leaves.

6. For rose, applique patterns A, B, C in that order.

7. Make rosebuds (see Folded Rosebud on page 7); applique in place.

8. Applique sepals, pattern E, in place.

Block Layout

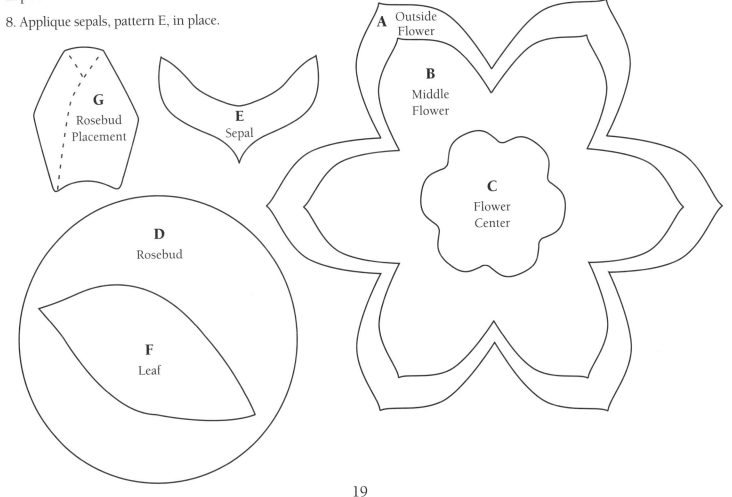

Peacock

Shown in color on page 24

This block has ten pattern pieces in addition to the bias strip stem and the little broderie perse flowers. For the broderie perse flowers, I simply cut some flowers from my theme fabric and appliqued them to the block. But, you can use a flower pattern from one of the other blocks to make your flowers or make up your own pattern.

Materials:

12 1/2" muslin square for background
assorted green fabrics for leaves
green bias strips for stems
theme fabric which has clusters of small flowers
2 shades of blue-green fabric for peacock's body and tail
3 blue fabrics for peacock's comb, wing and tail
yellow fabric for beak, legs, and tail
small piece of thin batting for wing
black permanent fine-point marking pen for eye
matching thread

Patterns:

A leaf, cut 15
B tail, cut 1
C lower feather, cut 5 yellow
D middle feather, cut 1 blue
E upper feather, cut 1 yellow
F beak, cut 1
G leg, cut 2
H body, cut 1
I wing, cut 1
J comb, cut 1

Instructions:

Note: See Basic Applique, page 5, before beginning to applique.

1. Trace pattern pieces onto template plastic (see Making Templates on page 4).

2. Mark design on background square (see Marking Background Fabric on page 4).

3. Cut out pattern pieces A through J from fabric adding 1/8" seam allowance all around.

4. Cut bias strip for stem (see Bias Strips on page 6). Applique in place. *Note: Since the short stem under the peacock's feet overlaps the long stem, it should be appliqued first.*

5. Applique leaves in place.

6. The peacock has different pieces appliqued on top of other pieces. Therefore, seam allowances hidden by another piece will not need to be finger pressed under. Applique lower tail (pattern B) in place. Re-mark pattern lines on tail as noted on pattern piece for patterns C and D on top of light blue-green fabric. *Note: When finger pressing areas that have inside points such as pattern B and pattern J, finger press past the inside point. Do the same on the other side of the inside point. Clip the point just before appliqueing the point down to keep raveling to a minimum.*

7. Applique feathers (pattern C) to lower tail.

8. Applique feathers (pattern D) in place. (See Note in step 6 above.)

9. Applique feathers (pattern E) in place. Re-mark pattern line for pattern H on top of yellow feather fabric.

10. Applique beak (pattern F) in place.

11. Applique back leg (pattern G) which will be overlapped by the body.

12. Applique body (pattern H) in place. It is important for the peacock's head and beak to join correctly. Adjustments may be made by removing the beak and replacing it at the proper place. Mark placement for wing on the peacock's body.

13. Applique front leg.

14. Applique comb. (See Note in step 6 above.)

15. Finger press seam allowances for wing (pattern I). Cut batting the exact finished size of wing. Place wing batting on

the back of the fabric wing inside the seam allowances; applique wing.

16. Applique small clusters of flowers cut from printed fabric in place (see Broderie Perse on page 9).

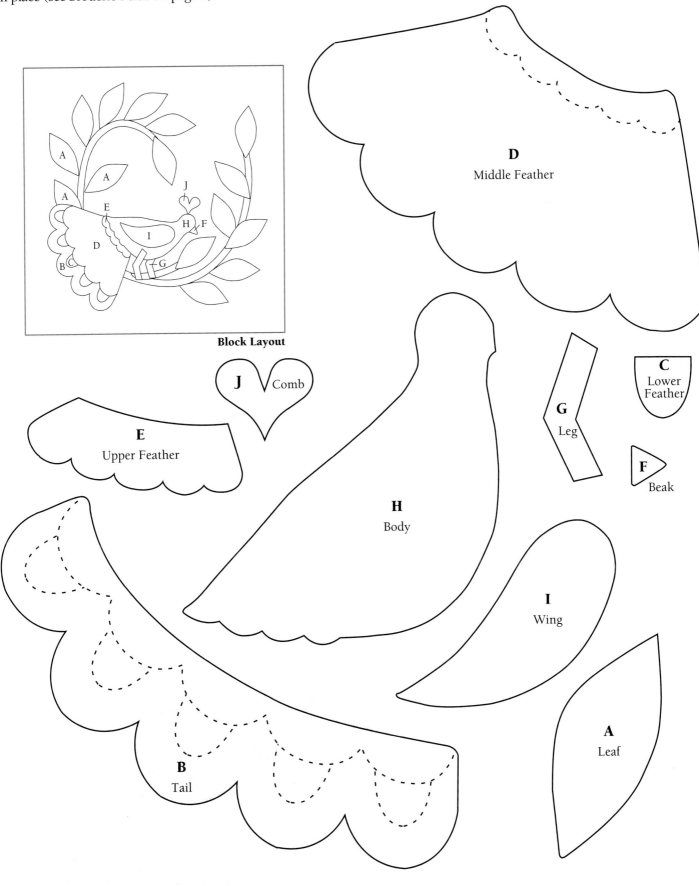

Block Layout

D
Middle Feather

C
Lower Feather

G
Leg

F
Beak

J Comb

E
Upper Feather

H
Body

I
Wing

A
Leaf

B
Tail

Holly Wreath

Shown in color on page 24

This simple block has three pattern pieces - a small holly leaf, a large holly leaf, and a circle for the yo-yo berry. The stem is a bias strip.

Materials:

12 1/2" muslin square for background
assorted green fabrics
red fabric for berries
theme fabric for stems
matching thread

Patterns:

A large leaf, cut 14
B small leaf, cut 7
C yo-yo, cut 7
D to-yo placement

Instructions:

Note: *See Basic Applique, page 5, before beginning to applique.*

1. Trace pattern pieces onto template plastic (see Making Templates on page 4).

2. Mark design on background square (see Marking Background Fabric on page 4). **Note:** *Use Pattern D to mark yo-yo placement on background square.*

3. Cut out pattern pieces A through C from fabric adding 1/8" seam allowance all around.

4. Make bias strips (see Bias Strips on page 6). Applique all stems in place; trim excess.

5. Applique all Pattern A leaves around outside of wreath and Pattern B leaves on inside of wreath. **Note:** *Be sure to begin applique at the point which will be hidden by a yo-yo.*

6. Make yo-yos (see Yo-Yos on page 6). Applique in place.

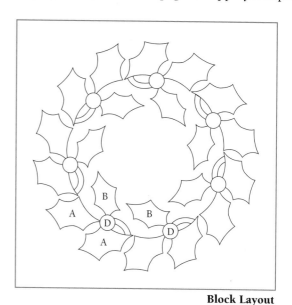

Block Layout

A
Large Leaf

B
Small Leaf

C
Yo-Yo

D
Yo-Yo Placement

Princess Feather

Rose of Sharon

Texas Bluebonnets

Bow-Tied Bouquet

Holly Wreath

Peacock

Basket of Pansies

Burgundy Flowers

Circle of Grapes

Cornucopia

Pink Thistle

Forget-Me-Not

Center Square

Outside Border

26

Basket of Pansies

Shown in color on page 24

The basket in this elegant block is made up entirely of bias strips. Ruched strips finish off the edges of the basket and the handle.

Materials:

12 1/2" muslin square for background

brown bias strips for body of basket

two 1" x 44" brown strips for ruched handle, bottom, and edge of basket

dk green bias strips for stems

assorted green fabrics for leaves

8 or 9 blue fabrics ranging from light to dark for pansies

yellow fabric for center of pansies

6 shades of pink to burgundy fabrics for berries (include theme fabric for lightest)

matching thread

Patterns:

A pansy bottom, cut 7

B pansy top, cut 7

C leaf, cut 8

D berry, cut 14

E pansy center, cut 7

Instructions:

Note: *See Basic Applique, page 5, before beginning to applique.*

1. Trace pattern pieces onto template plastic (see Making Templates on page 4).

2. Mark design on background square (see Marking Background Fabric on page 4).

3. Cut out all pattern pieces from fabric adding 1/8" seam allowance all around.

4. Cut brown bias strips for basket. Draw and cut accurately because it will be important to have all of the strips the same width. Applique strips starting from the outside toward the center; overlap strips at the bottom. **Note:** *You don't have to applique both edges of the bias strip if another strip is going to cover one of the edges. Applique center strip last.*

5. Because there is so much overlapping of leaves over pansies and pansies over leaves, it will be necessary to applique pieces in order. See **Fig 1** for applique sequence beginning with 1, 2, 3 and continuing to 40. When you come to the ruching in numbers 13, 24 and 25, see Ruching instructions on page 7. It is important that the ruching is done with "right angle" stitching so that it is even and the same width all along the strip. Do not tack as you go as with ruched flowers. **Note:** *The ends of 13 will be covered by 24 and 14. The left end of 24 will be tucked under then tacked in place before it is appliqued—the right end of 24 will be covered by 26. Both ends of 25 will be tucked under before it is appliqued.*

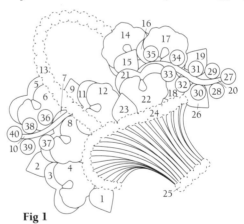

Fig 1

6. For the pansies, applique pansy top in place, stitching only the outer edge. Slip the pansy center (E) under the pansy top and applique the inverted "V" shape in the area over the yellow insert. Re-mark the pansy bottom pattern over the pansy top and yellow center. Applique pansy bottom in place. (In case you were wondering, two of the pansies are upside down!).

7. Applique berries last (see Flat Circles and Ovals on page 6). Note that the berries are colored from dark to light with the darkest ones at the tip.

continued

Forget-Me-Not

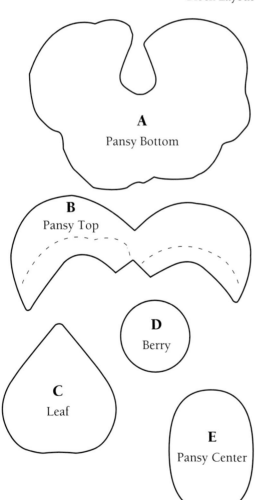

Block Layout

Shown in color on page 25

This block has four pattern pieces which include the blue flower, the leaf, the circular center of the flower, and the small yellow yo-yos which have been appliqued upside down to give the 3-dimensional effect.

Materials:

12 1/2" muslin square for background
assorted green fabrics
assorted blue fabrics
yellow fabric for yo-yos
"theme" (floral print) fabric for center of flowers
two brown fabrics for two leaves
8 cardboard circles for flower centers
spray starch
iron and ironing board
matching thread

Patterns:

A flower, cut 8
B leaf, cut 14
C flower center, cut 8
D yo-yo, cut 11
E yo-yo placement

A
Pansy Bottom

B
Pansy Top

D
Berry

C
Leaf

E
Pansy Center

continued

28

Instructions:

Note: *See Basic Applique, page 5, before beginning to applique.*

1. Trace pattern pieces onto template plastic (see Making Templates on page 4).

2. Mark design on background square (see Marking Background Fabric on page 4). Use Pattern E for marking yo-yo placement.

3. Cut out pattern pieces A through D from fabric adding 1/8" seam allowance all around.

4. It is important to applique pieces in sequence, **Fig 1,** since there is quite a bit of overlapping of petals over leaves, leaves over petals, and petals over petals.

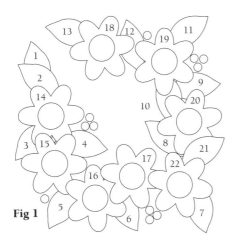

Fig 1

5. Make flower centers (see Flat Circle and Ovals, page 6); when completely dry remove cardboard and applique.

6. Make yellow yo-yos (see Yo-Yos page 6), but do not knot thread on the back; knot thread in the gathers on top. Turn the yo-yo over and applique face down to make the small stuffed flower.

Block Layout

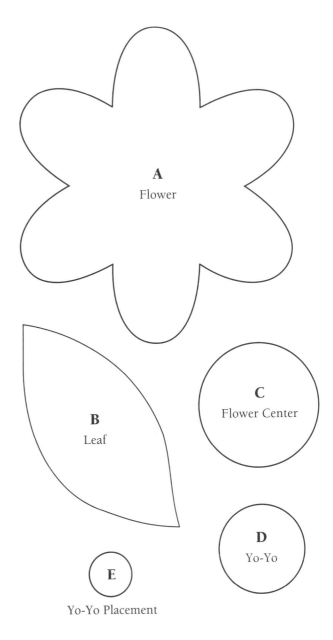

29

Pink Thistle

Shown in color on page 25

Ten pattern pieces make up this block; the bud, two sepal sizes, two leaf sizes, a small upside down yo-yo, two pieces for the larger pink flower, and two pieces of yellow for the reverse applique in the flower and bud. A bias strip is used for the stem.

Materials:

12 1/2" muslin square for background
assorted green fabrics for leaves and sepals
green bias strip for stems
yellow fabric for flowers
three or four different shades of pink fabric for flowers
   and buds
theme fabric for yo-yos
matching thread

Patterns:

A small leaf, cut 9 (3 are reversed)
B large leaf, cut 3
C thistle top, cut 3 (light pink)
D yellow piece for thistle, cut 3
E thistle bottom, cut 3 (dk pink)
F thistle sepal, cut 3
G bud, cut 3
H yellow piece for bud, cut 3
I bud sepal, cut 3
J yo-yo, cut 3
K yo-yo placement

Note: *Dotted lines on patterns C and G show placement for patterns D and H (yellow fabric for reverse applique), respectively.*

Instructions:

Note: *See Basic Applique on page 5 before beginning to applique.*

1. Trace pattern pieces onto template plastic (see Making Templates on page 4).

2. Mark design on background square (see Marking Background Fabric on page 4). Use Pattern K for marking yo-yo placement.

3. Cut out all pattern pieces from fabric adding 1/8" seam allowance all around. **Note:** *Cut six Pattern A leaves; flip pattern piece over and cut out three reversed leaves.*

4. Cut bias strip for stems (see Bias Strips on page 6). Applique all stems in place; trim excess.

5. Label each leaf on back of fabric since it is difficult to tell them apart. Applique pattern B leaves and reversed Pattern A leaves in center of block. Applique Pattern A leaves around outside edge. **Note:** *When finger pressing small curves as around the leaves, press about 1/8" at a time; clipping inside curves as you applique will also aid in making smooth curves.*

6. Baste yellow pieces for bud areas. (The buds will be appliqued over this yellow fabric so that only a small portion of the yellow will show.)
Re-mark outline of buds on top of the yellow fabric. Applique buds in place.

7. Baste yellow fabric for thistle areas. (The medium pink portions of the thistles will be appliqued over this yellow fabric so that only small portions of the yellow will show; therefore, you do not need to turn under seam allowance.) Re-mark outline of thistles on top of yellow fabric. Applique medium pink portions of the thistles in place.

8. Applique dark pink portions of the thistles in place; then applique sepals to bottoms of flowers.

9. Make yo-yos from light pink circles (see Yo-yos on page 6); knot thread on the front in the gathers of the yo-yo instead of on the back. Turn the yo-yo face down and applique in place on leaves.

Block Layout

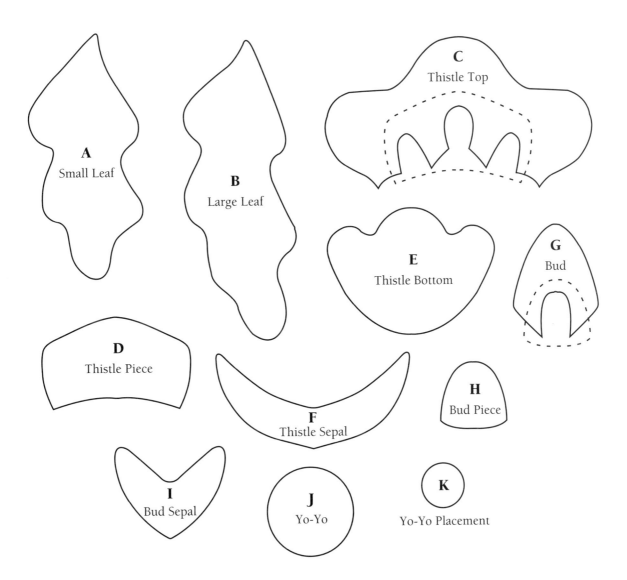

A
Small Leaf

B
Large Leaf

C
Thistle Top

E
Thistle Bottom

G
Bud

D
Thistle Piece

F
Thistle Sepal

H
Bud Piece

I
Bud Sepal

J
Yo-Yo

K
Yo-Yo Placement

Burgundy Flowers

Shown in color on page 24

The flower petal and leaf are the only two pattern pieces. There is a bias strip for the stem and seven additional strips for the ruched centers.

Materials:

12 1/2" muslin square for background
assorted green fabrics for leaves
green fabric for bias strip stems
two burgundy fabrics (one darker than the other) for
    flower petals
four 1" strips (cut crosswise) of theme fabric for
ruched centers—large multicolor or large two color
    prints also work well
matching quilting thread (for ruched centers)
matching thread

Patterns:

A petal, cut 26 burgundy and 9 darker burgundy
B leaf, cut 18
C ruched center placement

Instructions:

Note: See Basic Applique on page 5 before beginning to applique.

1. Trace pattern pieces onto template plastic (see Making Templates on page 4).

2. Mark design on background square (see Marking the Background Fabric on page 4). Use pattern C to mark ruched centers.

3. Cut out pattern pieces A and B from fabric adding 1/8" seam allowance all around.

4. Applique bias strips for stems (see Bias Strips on page 6).

5. The three leaves that overlap petals should not be appliqued at this time. Applique all other leaves.

6. The flower petals are divided into two groups: those that have a leaf or another petal overlapping and those that don't. The nine darker burgundy petals have a leaf or another petal overlapping them. Applique these petals first.

7. Applique the three leaves that overlap the dark burgundy petals.

8. Applique all light burgundy petals.

9. For the 1 1/4" flower centers, ruche light pink strips, using strong quilting thread. (See Ruching Instructions on page 7.) Applique in place.

Block Layout

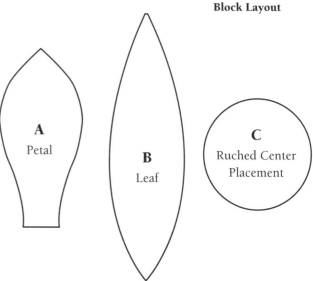

A
Petal

B
Leaf

C
Ruched Center
Placement

32

Cornucopia

Shown in color on page 25

This bountiful cornucopia is overflowing with lovely Irises, pretty ruched flowers and Folded Rosebuds.

Materials:

12 1/2" muslin square for background
5 shades of brown fabrics—from light to dark for cornucopia
dark green fabric for stems and bud stems
assorted green fabrics for leaves
4 pink to burgundy fabrics for ruched flowers and for buds
3 blue fabrics for iris
scraps of theme fabric for iris center
matching thread

Patterns:

A cornucopia top, cut 1
B cornucopia middle 1, cut 1
C cornucopia middle 2, cut 1
D cornucopia middle 3, cut 1
E cornucopia bottom, cut 1
F rosebud, cut 2
G iris, cut 3
H iris center, cut 3
I leaf, cut 9
J sepal, cut 2
K rosebud placement
L ruched flower placement

Instructions:

Note: See Basic Applique, page 5, before beginning to applique.

1. Trace pattern pieces onto template plastic (see Making Templates on page 4).

2. Mark design on background square (see Marking Background Fabric on page 4). Use Patterns K and L for marking placement of finished rosebuds and ruched flowers.

3. Cut out pattern pieces A through J from fabric adding 1/8" seam allowance all around. Note that the shading of the cornucopia goes from dark to light, therefore pattern A should be cut from the darkest brown fabric and Pattern E from the lightest.

4. Applique curnucopia using the light piece first, and continue until the darkest piece has been added.

5. Cut bias strips for stems (see Bias Strips on page 6). Applique in place.

6. Applique buds in place (see Folded Rosebuds on page 7).

7. Applique bud stems in place.

8. Applique all leaves in place.

9. Applique iris in place, then add yellow center.

10. Make ruched flowers (see Ruching on page 7). Applique in place.

Block Layout

continued

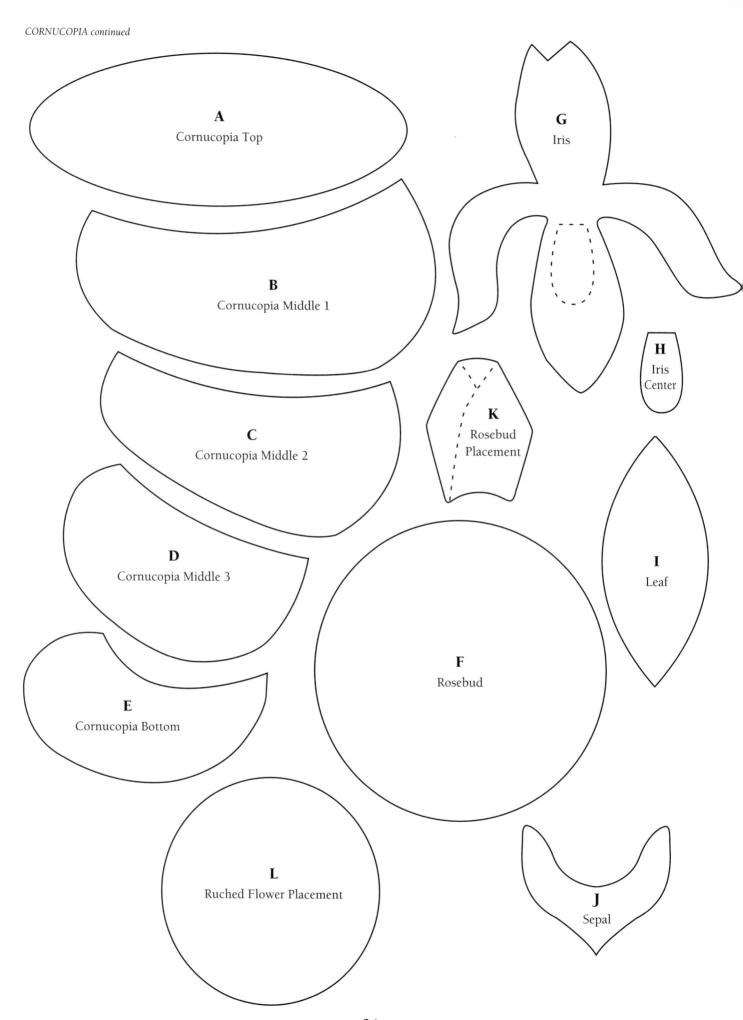

Circle of Grapes

Shown in color on page 25

This block has two pattern pieces, the circular grape and the grape leaf. The double grape vine is made with bias strips. Each grape is stuffed before being appliqued to the background.

Materials:

12 1/2" muslin square for background
2 shades of brown for grape vine bias strips (theme fabric for lighter strips)
assorted green fabrics for leaves
5 shades of blue fabrics (number fabrics 1 through 5 starting with the lightest as 1)
matching thread

Patterns:

A grape, cut 44
B leaf, cut 4
C grape placement

Instructions:

Note: *See Basic Applique, page 5, before beginning to applique.*

1. Trace pattern pieces onto template plastic (see Making Templates on page 4).

2. Mark design on background square (see Marking Background Fabric on page 4). Use Pattern C for marking grape placement.

3. Cut out pattern pieces A and B from fabric adding 1/8" seam allowance all around. Cut grapes using Pattern A as

follows: 4 from color 1; 8 each from colors 2 and 3; 12 each from colors 4 and 5.

4. Applique bias strips in place (see Bias Strips on page 6).

4. Applique leaves in place.

5. Make stuffed circles from blue circles and applique in place following numbers in **Fig 1** (see Stuffed Circles on page 7). Applique lightest blue grape at the end of the bias strip, getting progressively darker toward the vine, **Fig 1.**

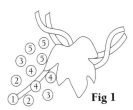

Fig 1

Block Layout

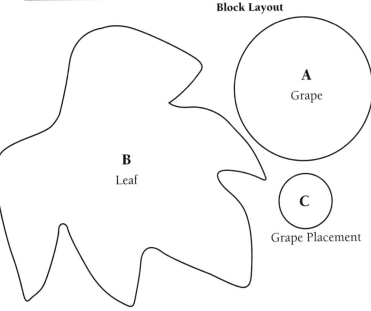

B
Leaf

A
Grape

C

Grape Placement

Bow Tied Bouquet

Shown in color on page 23

Two patterns are required for the tulips, two for the blue flowers, two for the bud and stem, three for the bow, one for the leaf, and two for the red flowers. The red flowers will be trapuntoed after being appliqued. A bias strip is used for the stems.

Materials:

12 1/2" muslin square for background
dk pink for tulip sides
theme fabric for tulip middle and trapunto flower centers
med pink fabric for buds
med blue for six-petal flowers
med aqua for centers of six-petal flowers
three shades of burgundy for trapunto
　flowers
scraps of yellow fabric for center of burgundy flowers
dk green bias strips for stems
assorted greens for leaves
green fabric for bud stems
lt aqua fabric for bow
matching thread
burgundy quilting thread to stitch trapunto design
small amount of polyester fiberfill

Patterns:

A tulip side, cut 6 (3 reversed)
B tulip middle, cut 3
C six-petal flower, cut 2
D flower center, cut 2
E trapunto flower, cut 3
F rosebud, cut 2
G right bow loop, cut 1
H left bow loop, cut 1
I left bow streamer, cut 1
J right bow streamer, cut 1
K bow knot, cut 1
L leaf, cut 5 (2 reversed)
M rosebud stem, cut 2
N trapunto flower center
O rosebud placement

Instructions:

Note: *See Basic Applique, page 5, before beginning to applique.*

1. Trace pattern pieces onto template plastic (see Making Templates on page 4).

2. Mark design on background square (see Marking Background Fabric on page 4). Use pattern O to mark placement of rosebud.

3. Cut out fabric pattern pieces A through N adding 1/8" seam allowance all around.

4. Cut bias strips for stems (see Bias Strips page 6). Applique in place; trim excess.

5. Applique leaves in place.

6. Make folded rosebuds (see Folded Rosebuds on page 7); applique in place.

7. Applique bud stems in place.

8. Applique bow loops, bow streamers and bow knot in place.

9. Applique tulip sides.

10. Applique tulip middles.

11. Applique six blue-petal flowers in place.

12. Applique med aqua circles for center of six-petal flowers (see Flat Circles and Ovals on page 6).

13. Applique dk burgundy flower in place. Overlap it with med burgundy flower. Overlap both with lt burgundy flower. Applique yellow centers to the flowers. Follow directions for Applique with Trapunto on page 8 to finish flowers. **Note:** *Just a little stuffing will do—overstuffing will cause the whole square to pucker.*

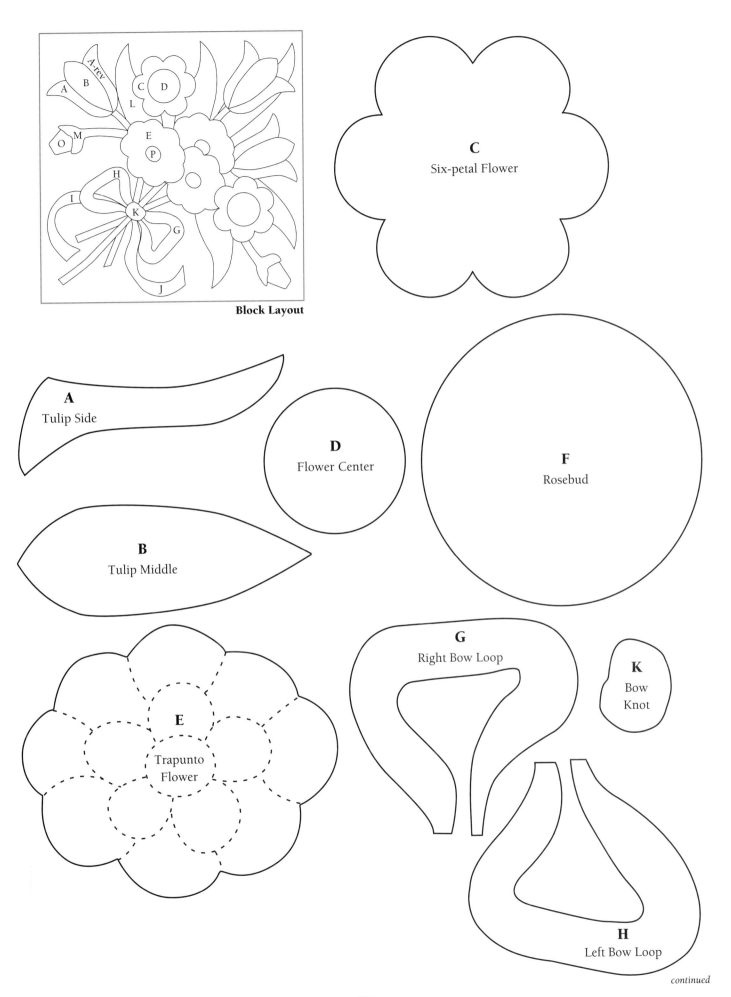

Block Layout

C
Six-petal Flower

A
Tulip Side

D
Flower Center

F
Rosebud

B
Tulip Middle

E
Trapunto
Flower

G
Right Bow Loop

K
Bow
Knot

H
Left Bow Loop

continued

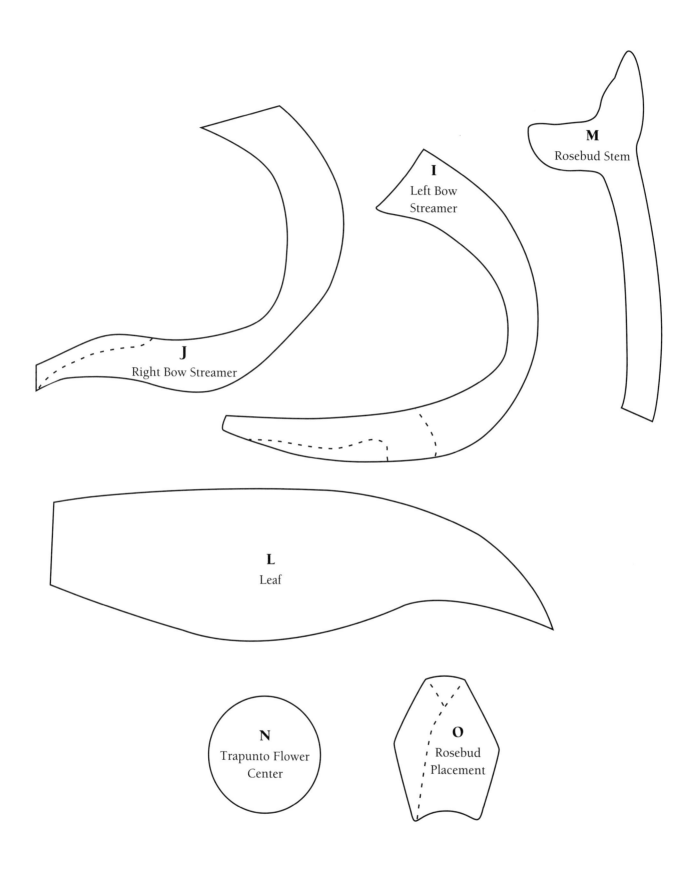

I
Left Bow
Streamer

M
Rosebud Stem

J
Right Bow Streamer

L
Leaf

N
Trapunto Flower
Center

O
Rosebud
Placement

Center Square

Shown in color on page 26

Materials:

34 1/2" muslin square for background

dk green fabrics for bias strip stems

assorted green fabrics for leaves

6 shades of burgundy fabric for berries (from light to dark)

5 shades of blue for Texas Bluebonnets

4 pink fabrics for rosebuds

four 1" x 42" strips of yellow fabric for yellow ruched flowers

scraps of theme fabric for center flower petals

scraps of blue fabric for center flower petals

one 1" x 42" strip of blue fabric for center ruched flower

assorted blue fabrics for iris, pansies, and six-petal flowers

scrap brown for center rosebud sepals

aqua print fabric for swags

four 2 1/2" x 36" strips of aqua print fabric for dogtooth border

matching thread

36" x 72" cardboard cutting board (optional, but very helpful)

Patterns and Cutting Requirements:

A petal, cut 4 blue and 4 theme fabric

B sepal, cut 4 brown

C rosebud, cut 12 pink

D pansy top, cut 3 light blue

E pansy bottom, cut 3 darker blue

F flower center, cut 3 light blue

G six-petal flower, cut 3 darker blue

H berry, cut 52 assorted burgundy

I large leaf, cut 44 assorted greens

J iris, cut 3 light blue

K iris center, cut 3 yellow

L small swag, cut 8 aqua print

M small leaf, cut 12 assorted greens

N short stem, cut 4 dark green

O long stem, cut 4 dark green

P Texas Bluebonnet placement

Q yellow ruched flower placement

R blue ruched center placement

S rosebud placement

T berry stem placement

U triangle for dogtooth border

Instructions:

Note: *See Basic Applique, page 5, before beginning to applique.*

1. Trace pattern pieces onto template plastic (see Making Templates on page 4).

2. Referring to Layout, **Fig 1** and **Fig 2,** as well as photograph, mark design including dogtooth border on background square (see Marking Background Fabric, page 4 and Dogtooth Border, page 10). **Fig 1** shows one corner of Center Square layout. **Fig 2** shows stem, leaf and bud placement at side points of swags.

Fig 1

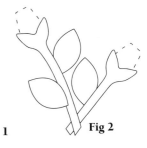
Fig 2

Note that each corner has a different blue flower. Therefore, mark the stems, leaves, rosebuds, and berries first in each corner, then add the correct blue flower.

3. Cut out pattern pieces A to O from fabric adding 1/8" seam allowance all around.

4. Cut bias strips from dark green for stems in center area of square (see Bias Strips, page 6). Applique in place; trim excess. Remember to applique short stems first, because longer stems will overlap them. Then applique large leaves in place.

continued

5. For center flower, applique four theme fabric petals first, then four blue petals. Ruche 1" x 42" strip for center and applique in place (see Ruching on page 7).

6. Applique pink rosebuds in place (see Folded Rosebud, page 7). Applique brown sepals over the buds.

7. Applique burgundy berries in the center section. Use darkest burgundy fabric for the end berry.

8. The blue flowers are appliqued around the outer circle of the central section. There are two pansies, two iris, two six-petal flowers, and four Texas Bluebonnets. Each set of flowers are found directly opposite each other. (Refer to photograph and block diagram for placement.) For more information on the Texas Bluebonnets, see page 17.

9. Applique small swags.

10. Applique dogtooth border around the outside of the center square (see Dogtooth Border, page 10).

11. At each swag corner, applique large leaves first, then bias stems. Applique berries in place, using dark burgundy at the tips of the stems and shading to lighter shades up the stems

12. Applique an iris, a pansy, a six-petal flower, and three Bluebonnets where the swags meet at each corner.

13. On each side where swags meet in center, applique rosebuds first (see Folded Rosebuds, page 7), then short and long stems, and finally small leaves.

14. Make four yellow ruched flowers (see Ruching, page 7). Applique in place where the swags meet in the center of each side. ***Note:*** *Make sure to cover the stem that comes up from the center of the block.*

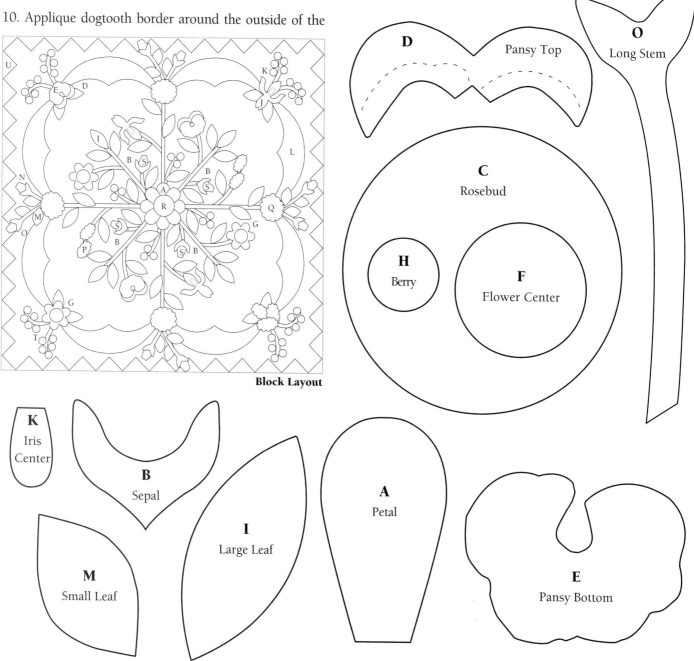

Block Layout

40

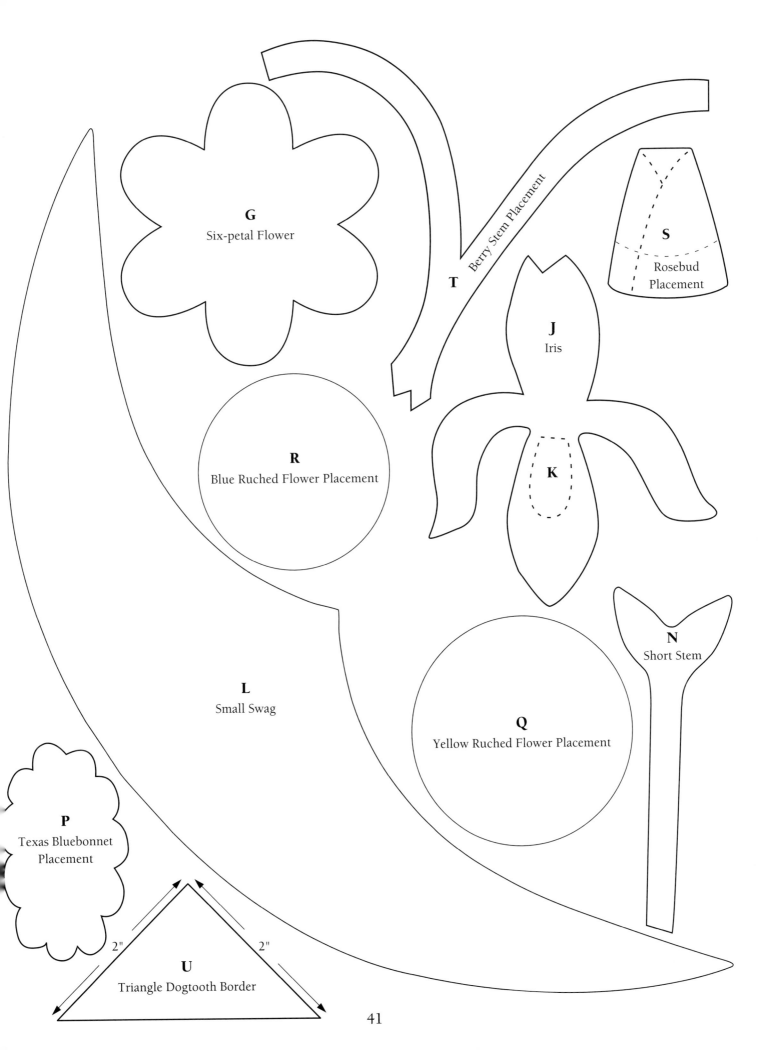

G
Six-petal Flower

T

Berry Stem Placement

S
Rosebud
Placement

J
Iris

R
Blue Ruched Flower Placement

K

N
Short Stem

L
Small Swag

Q
Yellow Ruched Flower Placement

P
Texas Bluebonnet
Placement

2"   2"

U
Triangle Dogtooth Border

Outside Borders

Shown in color on page 26

Materials:

four 12" x 96" strips of background fabric
eight 2 1/2" x 96" strips aqua print fabric for
    dogtooth border
aqua print fabric for 16 large size swags
aqua print fabric for 4 corner swags
assorted green fabrics for leaves
dk green fabrics for bias strips for stems
dk green fabrics for bud stems
assorted light to dark shades of pink/burgundy fabrics
    for berries
six pink fabrics for rosebuds
assorted blue fabrics for iris, pansies, six-petal flowers,
    and Texas Bluebonnets
matching thread

Other Supplies:

water soluble marking pen

Patterns:

A berry, cut 112 assorted burgundy
B small leaf, cut 36 assorted greens
C large leaf, cut 40 assorted greens
D six-petal flower, cut 2 dark blue
E flower center, cut 2 med blue
F pansy top, cut 2 light blue
G pansy bottom, cut 2 dark blue
H iris, cut 2 light blue
I iris center, cut two light blue
J rosebud, cut 24 assorted pinks
K short bud stem, cut 12 dark green
L long bud stem, cut 12 dark green
M large swag, cut 16 (on fold) aqua print
N corner swag, cut 4 (on fold) aqua print
O dogtooth border triangle for placement
P rosebud placement
Q ruched flower placement
R Texas Bluebonnet placement
S rosebud stem placement
T grape stem placement

Instructions:

Note: *See Basic Applique, page 5, before beginning to applique.*

1. Trace pattern pieces onto template plastic (see Making Templates on page 4).

2. Referring to photograph and Fig 1 for placement, mark design, including dogtooth border, on background strips (see Marking Background Fabric, page 4 and Dogtooth Border, page 10). Mark mitered corners on end of each border. **Note:** *Opposite borders are identical.*

Fig 1

3. Cut out pattern pieces A to N from fabric, adding 1/8" seam allowance all around.

4. Applique dogtooth border (see Dogtooth Border, page 10).

5. Applique large swags.

6. Applique large leaves where swags meet.

7. Applique bias strips for berry stems.

8. Applique berries, using darker berries at the end of the stems and lighter berries up the stem.

9. Applique pink rosebuds, bud stems and small leaves.

10. Applique two blue flowers on each side of the outside border. If using Texas Bluebonnets (see Texas Bluebonnets, page 17) make three together. Photographed quilt has an iris and six-petal flower on two strips and a pansy and three Texas Blue Bonnets on the other two strips.

11. Make twelve yellow ruched flowers, three for each side. Applique one flower to the middle of each border at this time.

12. The remaining eight yellow ruched flowers and corner swags will be appliqued after the quilt top has been sewn together. (See Finishing the Quilt, page 48.)

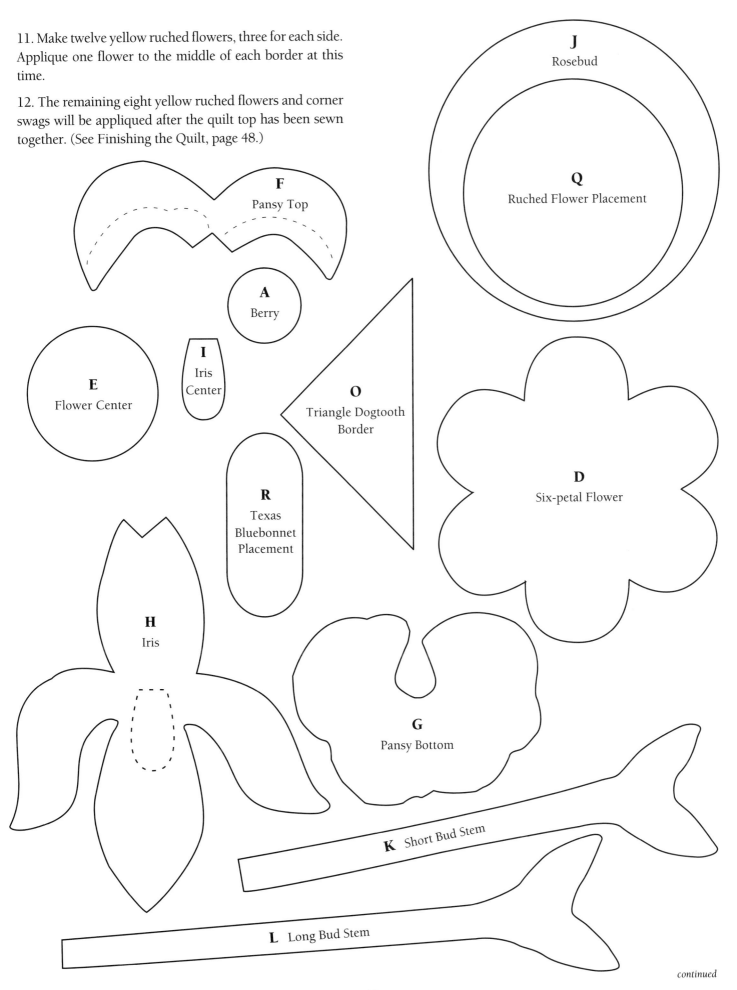

F Pansy Top

J Rosebud

Q Ruched Flower Placement

A Berry

E Flower Center

I Iris Center

O Triangle Dogtooth Border

D Six-petal Flower

R Texas Bluebonnet Placement

H Iris

G Pansy Bottom

K Short Bud Stem

L Long Bud Stem

continued

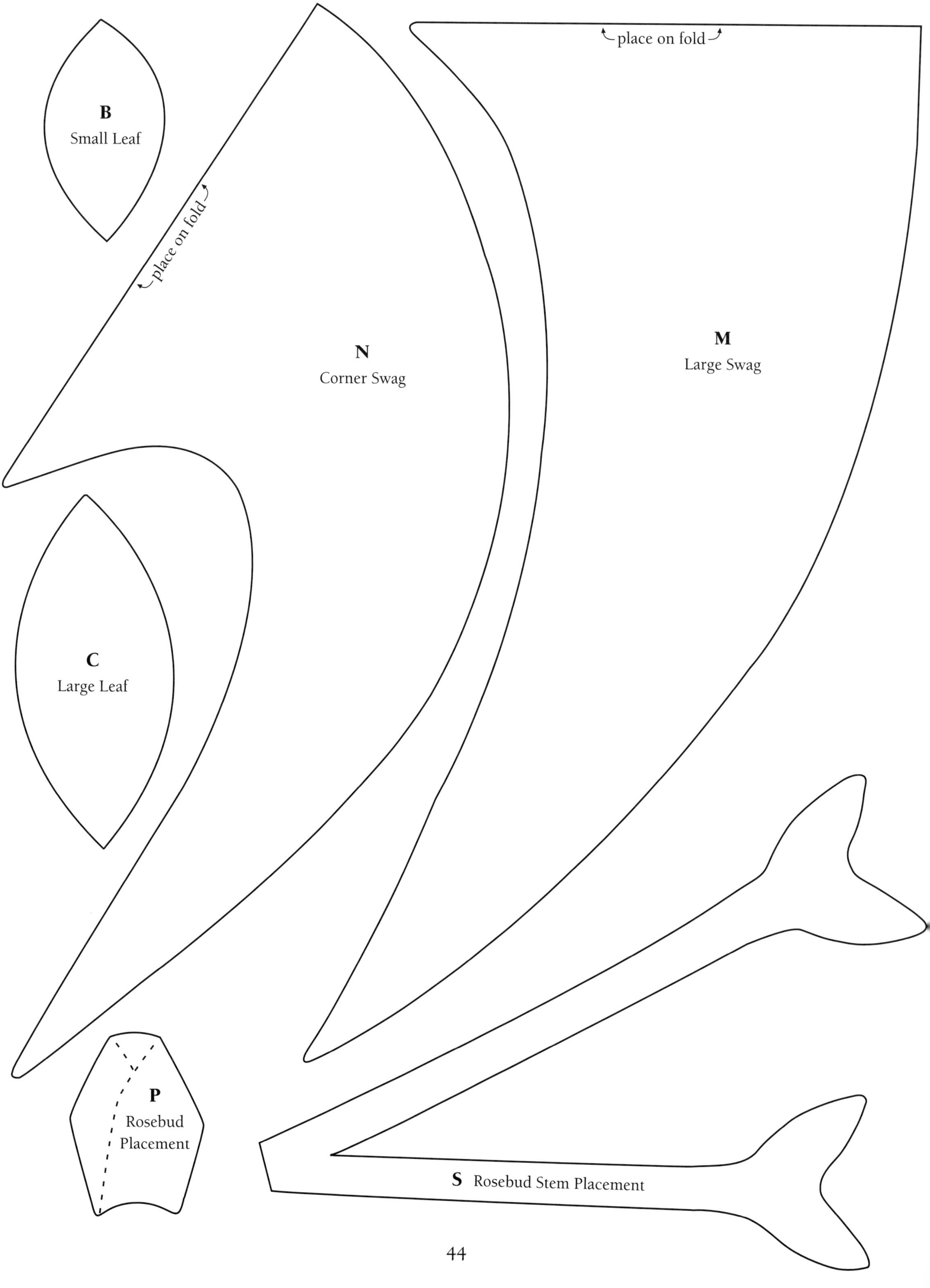

B
Small Leaf

↵ place on fold ↩

N
Corner Swag

↵ place on fold ↩

M
Large Swag

C
Large Leaf

P
Rosebud
Placement

S Rosebud Stem Placement

44

Leaf Quilting Pattern Placement
near Small Swags on Center Square

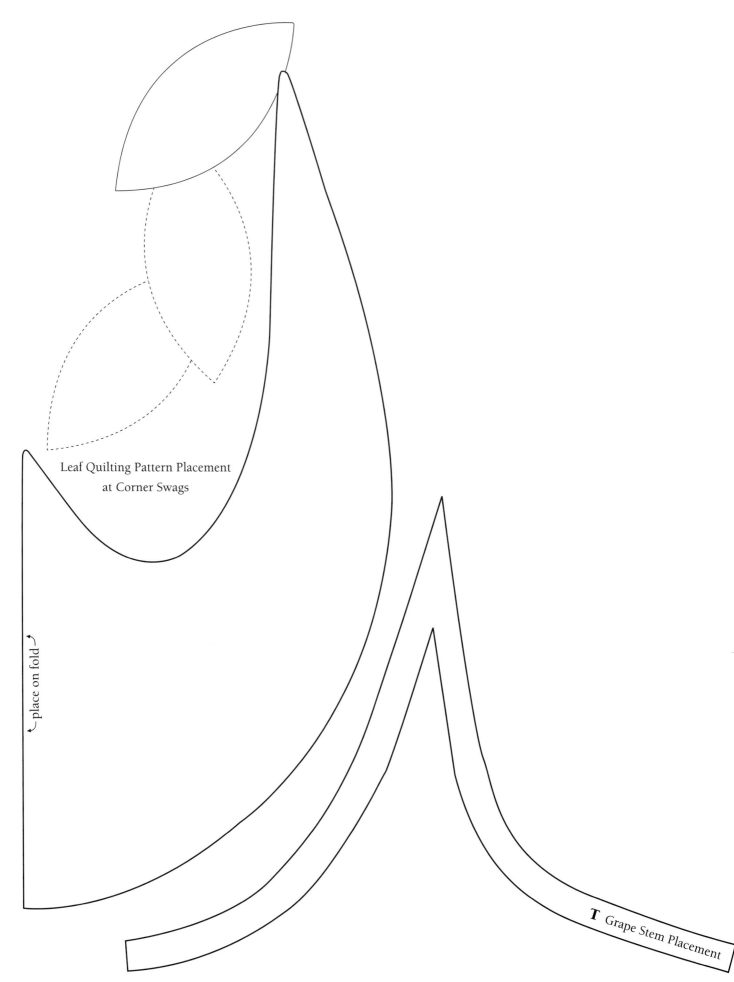

Leaf Quilting Pattern Placement
at Corner Swags

← place on fold ↩

T Grape Stem Placement

46

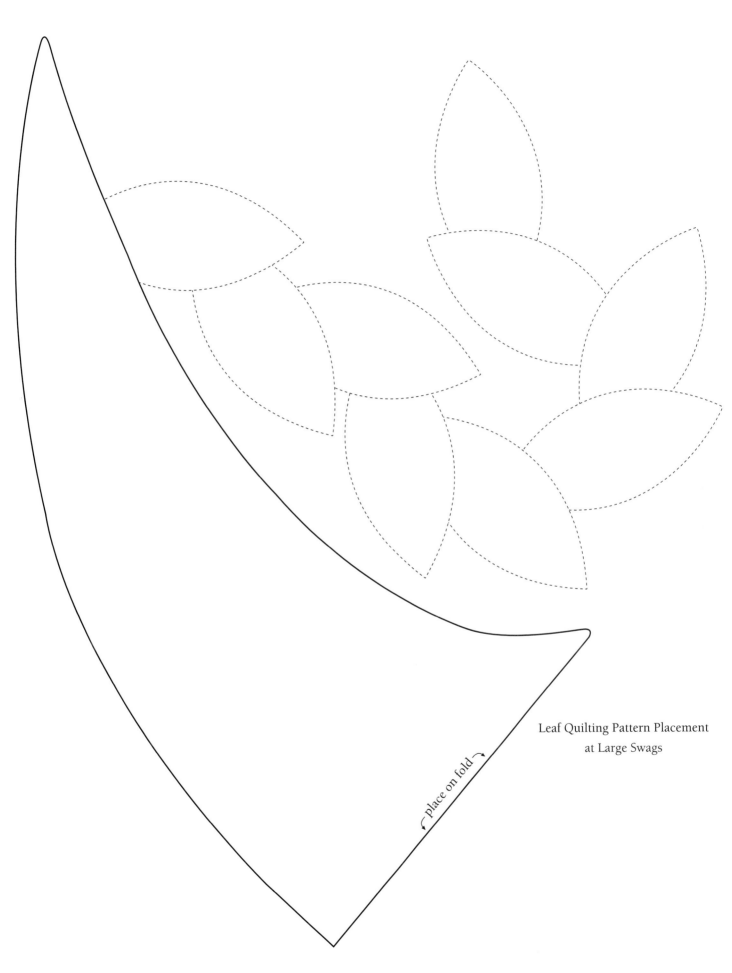

Leaf Quilting Pattern Placement
at Large Swags

place on fold

Finishing Your Quilt

Completing the Quilt Top

1. Referring to layout as well as photographs on covers for placement, arrange appliqued blocks, appliqued center square, pieced triangles (from section on Piecing and Attaching the Sawtooth Border, page 10), and borders on the floor.

2. Sew Princess Feather block (1) to a pieced A Triangle along the lower left side. Sew another pieced A Triangle along the lower right side of the block. Sew a pieced A Triangle to upper left side and lower left side of Bow-tied Bouquet (2). Sew a pieced A Triangle to upper right and upper left of the Basket block (3) and sew a pieced A Triangle to upper right and amother one to lower right of the Cornucopia block (4). Sew all four sections to center block, **Fig 1.**

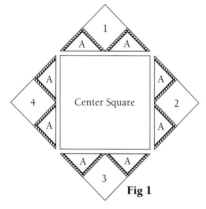

Fig 1

3. For corner section, sew two pieced B Triangles together, **Fig 2.** Sew a pieced A Triangle to an appliqued block, add another block and another pieced A Triangle, **Fig 3.** Sew the two units together, **Fig 4.**

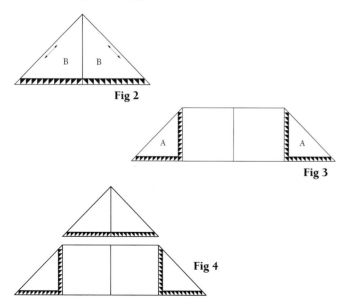

Fig 2

Fig 3

Fig 4

4. Repeat step 3 for the three remaining corner sections noting position of blocks as you sew. Sew the corner sections to corners of center block, **Fig 5.**

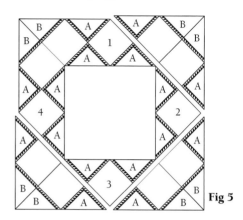

Fig 5

5. Sew each outside border to each side of the quilt, making sure that dogtooth and sawtooth borders match, **Fig 6.** Miter corners by sewing on the lines drawn when marking borders. Applique corner swags over the mitered corners and applique the rest of yellow ruched flowers where swags meet.

Fig 6